Green Snake
on a
Green Grass

ALSO BY NGOZI OLIVIA OSUOHA

The Transformation Train
Letter to My Unborn
Sensation
Tropical Escape (with Amos O. Ojwang')
Fruits from the Poetry Planet
Poetic Grenade
Whispers of the Biafran Skeleton
Chains
Raindrops
Freeborn
Eclipse of Tides
The Subterfuge

Green Snake on a Green Grass

poems by
Ngozi Olivia Osuoha

Poetic Justice Books
Port St. Lucie, Florida

©2019 Ngozi Olivia Osuoha

book design and layout: SpiNDec, Port Saint Lucie, FL
cover image: *Green Party*, ©2019 Kris Haggblom

All rights reserved.

No part of this book may be used or reproduced in any manner whatsoever without written permission except in the case of brief quotations embodied in critical articles and reviews. Members of educational institutions and organizations wishing to photocopy any of the work for classroom use, or authors, artists and publishers who would like to obtain permission for any material in the work, should contact the publisher.

Published by Poetic Justice Books
Port Saint Lucie, Florida
www.poeticjusticebooks.com

ISBN: 978-1-950433-33-9

FIRST EDITION
10 9 8 7 6 5 4 3 2 1

This book is dedicated to all the people who have died an unnecessary death especially in Nigeria. Deaths, that could have been prevented. The deaths that were directly or indirectly aided by powers that should have saved them.

contents

Theorem 3
Law 4
Principles 5
Equations 6
Constitution 7
The Rule 8
Stipulation 9
Code 10
Power 11
Bond 12
Promises 13
Creeds 14
Motto 15
Questions 16
Lies 17
Roadblocks 18
Herdsman 19
Bandits 20
Kidnappers 21
Uniforms 22
Insecurity 23
Time Bomb 24
Traces of War 25
Politicians 26
Governance 27
Media 29
Trumpeters 30
Whistle Blowers 31
Intimidation 32
Injustice 33
Contracts 34
Connection 35
Allocation 36
Green Snake 37
Manifesto 38
Thugs 39

Family on Cruise Control 40
Trouble 42
Green Grass 43
National Cake 44
Pretenders 46
Oil 47
Blind 48
Agriculture 49
Industries 50
Unemployment 51
Cartel 52
Scholarship 53
False Contracts 54
Titles 55
Commissioning Fake Projects 56
Rented Crowds 57
Old Stuffs 58
Hiring 59
Immunization 60
Negligence 61
Incompetence 62
Arraigning Fake Suspects 63
Detention 64
Crime Is Business 65
Syndicates 67
Rituals 68
Bribery and Corruption 69
Pregnancy 70
False Diagnosis 71
Sorting and Sexual Harassment 72
Diseases 73
Drivers and Guards 74
Cooks and Maids 75
Visas 76

Green Snake on a Green Grass

THEOREM

Green snake on a green grass
White dove in a white cloud
Dazzling sword on a shiny glass
A lunatic in a madding crowd.

Black wall in darkness
Red coat covering blood,
Blue rain painting the sky
White robe teaching cleanliness
Dirty water supporting flood
Faint voice pretending to cry.

Ngozi Olivia Osuoha

LAW

As if the law is satanic
Spilling evil and barbaric
Laws propelling harm
Opposing freedom and charm.

A law so raw
With a long claw
Yet nothing good it does draw.

Law, for the lawless
Lawless people Manning the law
Law, lowering the guards.

Laws against poor people
Law for rich people
Law, supporting
Law, dehumanizing.

Laws, tight and rigid
Porous yet, cancerous still
Laws, antagonizing
Yet, fronting goodness and mercy.

PRINCIPLES

Laid principles
In such disciplines
Basking for ruins
Sparing not penguins.

Principles of doom
On a windy room
Beheading the groom
Sweeping blood with broom
And turning all; gloom.

Principles of men
Releasing semen
Drowning seamen
Breaking hymen
Burning pen
Burying them in a den.

Principles of hate
Cheering probate
Applauding reprobate
Dark principles of fate.

Ngozi Olivia Osuoha

EQUATIONS

Equations of evil
Subtracting by the devil
Multiplying deaths
Adding to their wealth.

Equations of severe pain
Substituting of dry pain
Eliminating the rain
Brackets of stain
Hallowing vain.

Equations of empirical formula
Harmonizing periodical bacteria
Matching historical particulars
Binding conical spatulas,
Venting sutures of coma
Lording nurtures of dilemma.

Equations that delude
Illusive equations that betray
Captivating postulates
That contradict and contravene.

CONSTITUTION

It is as if the constitution is dead
Making gain for the head
It is as though it is fake
Yearning only against the lake
It satisfies their make
Elevating their rake,
Tormenting at wake
Poisoning the cake
Like an earthquake
It dies for poor-sake
That seems their take.

The constitution is a paper
It sounds very proper
Distinct like the harper
But actually against the pauper.

Ngozi Olivia Osuoha

THE RULE

They rule the role
And position the pole
They tear the sole
And control the soul
The rule, they rule, is a misrule.

Hard rule, harsh rule
Struggle and jungle
Hustle and puzzle
Ruling the weak
Misruling the poor
Rules that rule from unruly people.

STIPULATION

They stipulate their goal
And fix their interest
They enact their wish
And write their will,
They speculate and stipulate.

Their choice is the rule
Their dream is the law
Their need is the constitution.

Their aim is the environment
Their target is the foundation,
They end up in harm and pain
The people bear the brunt of all their game.

Ngozi Olivia Osuoha

CODE

A cabal of set creed
Working to upload it
A fraternity of definite faith
Fighting to defend it
In all honour, and honesty
In all integrity and capacity
In unified unity and strength
Of unrelenting love and passion
Coded and imbeded in shrines
Enshrined in oaths and covenants
Codes, slogans, creeds and articles
Motto, pledges, loyalties and commitments
Green snake on a green grass,
A piece of unwanted labour.

POWER

Spirit of infinite zeal
Haunting for performance
Parading quest and lust
Insinuating discourse of ill
Dividing to rule
Ruling to divide
Rule and divide
Division, connivance, nuisance.

Power of hate, power of anger
Power of bitterness, power of lust
Power of dominance, power of greed
Selfish lot, cooking self-pot
Vengeful breed, green grass
The green snake that deceives.

Ngozi Olivia Osuoha

BOND

A great bond
Deep, deeper, deepest
As far as the abyss
Sharing things in common
A bond that knows no boundary.

The green snake is a bond
The bond on green grass
Bearing boundless boundaries
Conceiving, deceiving, collaborating
Cohorts of wondrous thunders
Thunderous lightnings of high sounds
Sounding louder and farther
Incapacitating dreams of poor minds
Thwarting hopes of lifeless visions
A green snake on a green grass,
Nations of deceptive foundation.

PROMISES

Promises of bitterness
Lies from the pit of hell
They promise heaven and earth
And heaven on earth
They end up making earth, a hell.

Yes, the poor earth
They make it hell
They bring hell upon earth
And destroy earth
Because they are immortals.

Promises of impossibilities
Full of sweet words
Sweet words of total deception
Deceptions of agony and libidos.

The green grass housing green snake
Green snake hiding on green grass
A deep subterfuge, bondage of greed.

Green promises, serpentine promises
Green like forest and vegetation
As if they are fertile.

Ngozi Olivia Osuoha

CREEDS

Creeds of greed
Greediness of greenness
Embodied in creeds
They idolize fame
And bury shame,
They blame, blame and blame
Their game has no name
They play, play and play
Yet they are so lame.

Creeds of unconscious breed
Dead conscience, dead soul
Dead future, dead name
They immortalize their shame
And part all not involved.

Creeds of sacred-less covenants
Covenants of ungodly union,
Green snake on a green grass
Biting, poisoning, killing.

MOTTO

Their motto is strong
Stronger than pain
The pain of the people.

They live in a cycle
Their cycle never cuts
It rotates, revolves and circulates
It rolls over to the unborn.

Motto of indecent rule
Watchwords of inhumane practises
Beliefs of ungodly attitudes
Principles of unruly kingdoms
Exaggerating, excavating, exhuming
Emptying, employing, elongating evil.

A set of daredevils
Breeding torture and torment
Crucifying glory and nailing honour
The motto of subterfuge
Green motto of a green snake
Reflecting pain and poison
Venoms of horrible snake
Bitter prism of hardened criminality.

Ngozi Olivia Osuoha

QUESTIONS

The questions wonder yonder
As even the younger wonders
Green venoms, pure green.

Questions baffling the wise
Confusing the great
Bothering the giant,
Green snake poisoning the green grass.

Questions of numberless answers
Yet no answers to numberless questions
Questions that surprise the old
And trouble the young,
When shall all these cease
And peace and tranquil reign again?

Poisoned land overflowing with venoms
Snakes, grasses of dry venom.

LIES

Calculated lies
Properly instigated
Accurately incited
Proportionally induced
Lies, simple, hard, crude.

Lies, glaring lies
Lies, white lies
Daily, weekly, monthly, quarterly, annually
Told openly and secretly
Without shame, fear, conscience
Trying to conceal clear truth.

Lies, green, black, crystal
Bitter lies, sweet lies
Little and big lies
Unfair lies, inhumane lies
Lies children dare not tell
The green snake, hiding in the the grass.

Ngozi Olivia Osuoha

ROADBLOCKS

As they mount roadblocks
In the name of checkpoints
Checking and collecting
Collecting monies and lives
Taking whatever they can.

Roadblocks and checkpoints
Submitting quotas and offerings
Making millions for masters
As masters shout on screens
Trying to deceive the people
Pretending to be ordering off roadblocks.

Green snake, green grass
Greenness, a loud pretence
Obvious and conspicuous.

HERDSMEN

Now, it is herdsmen
Killing and slaughtering
Butchering and burying
Invading and conquering
Killing, maiming, raping, murdering.

Scores, skulls, sores and sacrileges
Abominations, taboos, desecration
Shattering, scatterings, destructions
Bloodthirsty touts, illiterate slaves
Uncultured extremists, unafrican maggots
Drinking blood, blood of the Innocent
Blood of green future, and green hope.

Snakes and pythons
Crippling agents crippling the society
Serpentine locusts and swampy evil
Out for blood, nothing but blood.

Herdsmen that value cows
Honouring and serving cattle
Loving and sleeping with animals
Replacing men with cows
Making provisions for them and starving men
Raping souls and whipping spirits
Scrapping, clearing altars
Altars and shrines of African and godly cultures.

Ngozi Olivia Osuoha

BANDITS

Bandits in new regalia
Sweeping the highways
Attacking all and sundry
Killing, raping and vanquishing.

Assaults and assault rifles
Guns, machetes and axes
Weapons of different kinds
Destroying men and women
Traumatizing the nation.

Acting as though with backups
Informants, information
Proofs, guns and bullet proofs
Supplies and supply chains
Victims of degradation and poor governance.

Green venoms from green snake on green grass
Crawling to harm a people
A people of powerless will.

KIDNAPPERS

Lions in den
Wolves amidst sheep
Killers among shepherds
Kidnappers, within and without.

Evil of desperate order
Orders of despicable evil
Smoke, choking the land
A choking smoke
A land of unequalled trouble
Melting and slipping away
On a slide of slanted fate
Jiggling and giggling
As if a jingle amuses them all.

Kidnappers of unparalleled effrontery
Terrorizing the peace of the people
Terminating lives, unfortunate victims
Restless abode of helpless masses
Tormenting funnel of legless runners
Cloudy world of voiceless prayers
Exceeding terror upon a lifeless land.

Green oil of daring strength
Strengthening snakes of diverse venom
Biting and killing,
Swallowing, and defecating on families.

Ngozi Olivia Osuoha

UNIFORMS

Uniforms everywhere
Intimidating the mufti
Ripping and stripping it
Flogging, beating, murdering
Sending it to hell, unannounced.

Uniforms against uniforms
Discouraging brotherhood and sportsmanship
Corking, shooting, triggering, stray bullets
Killing with joy, pride and passion
Wasting green lives uncontrollably
Cleansing ethnically and technically
Unchecked, uncautioned, unarrested.

Pure green, dark green, sea green, army green
All greenness, green ocean of blood
Green snake, green grass
Venom on land.

INSECURITY

Development is dead
Investors are gone
Profit is loss
Loss is profit,
Nothing is working
All is at a standstill
Everything is burning out.

Insecurity on the rise
As though it has a boost
Crystal and glaring like daylight
Fear looms, doom glows.

Industries are packing
Workers are hungry
Pensioners are dying
The state is flat
Flatter than ground
Nothing seems to be alive
The green and greenness drying up
Yet the green grass hiding the green snake.

Ngozi Olivia Osuoha

TIME BOMB

They say it is dark
Dark, darkness like night
Like a keg of gunpowder
A time bomb set to explode
To explode at the detriment of all.

Powers and the powers that be
Rulers and rulers that rule,
Misrulers and misleaders
Misguidance and misgovernment
Approaching point of no return
Helter skelter, spirits and ghosts
From pillar to post, humans and beasts.

Running from the green snake
Running to meet yet the green grass
The green grass he has poisoned,
Uncertainties, unbelievable and unthinkable.

TRACES OF WAR

No war is on
But war is on,
Killings up and down
Murders front and back,
Bombs and suicide bombings
Churches, mosques, markets, schools, parks
Dozens and hundreds all the time.

Gunshots, attacks, grenades
Sophisticated weapons with the enemy
Like godfathers pumping champagnes
Partying at news of deaths.

Terrorism, racism, tribalism, segregation
Marginalization, ethnic cleansing, one-sided appointments
Political interest of keen discrimination,
Blunt tribal remarks and hate speeches
Shutting others down, killing and attacking a particular people
Camouflaging leadership, sabotaging unity
Subterfuge in dark shades
Judas, kisses of Judas's betrayal.

Green snake biting national cake
Poisoning it for patriots,
Parading victims as suspects
Charging mourners and weepers.

Ngozi Olivia Osuoha

POLITICIANS

They are there for themselves
Fighting against themselves,
Protecting each other yet
As the country burns.

They loot, steal, divide
Sitting on rules, laws and answers
Blunt, unsharpened and unbroken.

Allocations, appropriations, salaries and allowances
Unimaginable investments home and abroad
Foreign medical trips, partners, players and plays
Studies, works, luxuries abroad;
To hell with the masses.

They breed and brew hell here
Fomenting trouble, hate and fight
Instigating enmity, causing mayhem
The jobless youths and hungry masses
A camouflage of leaders for them.

Green snakes, they are the venom
Green snakes, they are the snake
Green snakes, they are the grass
Green snakes, they are the wildfire.

GOVERNANCE

The opposite of peace and joy
The abuse of power
The misuse of passion
The misplacement of priorities
Governance, a hell on earth.

Governing a people of diverse cultures
Imposing your wants on them
Forcing your logic down their throat
Threatening their peace and rights
Luring them to succumb.

Governance, a rope of mysterious strength
Trapping and weaving gaints
Tracing and trading legends
Trapping and tolling heroes,
Poisoning the land against the unborn.

Far from peace, far beyond unity
Away from development, outside progress
Behind science and technology, hidden
Frustrating the land, killing the earth
Maiming the future, murdering growth
Taming pride, intoxicating dreams
Governance, a pit of bottomless wonders
Cooking meals of unsatisfactory flavour
Dishing forcefully on citizenry.

Cutting off hands, hands of labour
Endangering species, species of mighty breed
Governance, an advanced torture.

Ngozi Olivia Osuoha

Forcing people to violently cohabit
Compelling lions and tigers to coexist
Wishing away pain, igniting violence
Rekindling anger, anger of boredom
Building flames of fires that raze
Razing skyscrapers of divine anointing.

Governance, a deceit, a camouflage
A pan of painful breeze
Hurricanes of windy fire, wildfire
Burning, destroying, razing, scrapping
Shutting down lives and nations
Gathering ashes and skulls for rituals
Instituting barriers, loud boundaries of death.

Green snake flying up
Dancing beneath, crawling down
Green grass of hardened herbs
Carnivorous reptile of perpetual harm.

MEDIA

They hijack the media
And give it a voice
A voice singing their glory
Painting them as angels.

Nobody questions nor challenges
No other news is relevant
Suppression, oppression, depression, frustration.

The media meditates on them
Marries and massages their ego
Caresses and manages their body,
Quiet and calm on other issues
Blind and silent to realities
Pretending as if all is well.

Threats and targets
Fears canvassing for headship
Sermons and worships
Worshippers and glorifiers
The media swallows terror
Even in the face of excruciating pain.

Ngozi Olivia Osuoha

TRUMPETERS

Trumpeters of numerous gifts
Converging to honour evil
Fluters and harpers of pure voices;
Conveying great tunes
Of high frequencies and straight pitch
Melodies and melodious music in perfect rhythm
Pipers and dancers of raw zeal
Beckoning on spirits to manifest
To manifest manifold miracles,
Miraculous weight upon a troubled lot
Confused and mesmerized lot.

Never thinking of humanity
Portraying red as green
And black as white,
Standing on skulls to dance
A dance of blood
Candid soloists, puzzling the dead.

Courage of mere bewilderment
Perfection of evil
Shaming souls of the faithful departed.

Green snake, concerts of highly empowered deceit
Concerts of painful performance
Covering graves, mass innocent graves.

WHISTLE BLOWERS

whistle blowers blowing dusty wind
Raising false alarms
Twisting stories and news
Rumourmongers, rumouring
Fighting for selfish gains
Roping in, the Innocent.

Whistlers and blowers of harm
Harmful chains of deadly agents
Contradicting, contravening and camouflaging
Cooking unpalatable meals
Dishing out woeful banquets
Relaxing on hunting heads.

Whistle blowers, paid servants
People exhuming stories from unexisting grounds
Scavengers, sycophants and black sheep
Wayward groups and godless tables
Mean and unscrupulous elements
Blowing loud and noisy whistles
Defaming, deforming, assassinating characters
Determined to pull down.

Green snake, long and dreary
Scary grass, green as though alive.

Ngozi Olivia Osuoha

INTIMIDATION

Using forces to intimidate the populace
Arresting agitators
Bullying protesters
Compelling others to be quiet.

Uniforms abusing tools
Working against the people
Intimidating opinions
Shutting down movements
Forcing everyone to bend or break.

Intimidations, guns and agents
Locking all inside a container
The content notwithstanding,
Blocking air, and blocking reach.

Green snake of most dangerous venom
Poison of non-curable disease
Spreading, and encroaching.

INJUSTICE

Slow judiciary and legal system
Injustice mounting pressure
Working with boldness.

Atrocities fanning hate
Sacrileges booming anger
Sabotage, delay, frustrations and failures
Cooking against the poor.

Evil doers go freely
Perpetrators never brought to book
Investigations inconclusive
Unheard results, unknown figures
Cement cementing truth.

Money buying freedom
Riches purchasing justice
Wealth suppressing speech
Terror killing religion
Injustice flying with wings
Spreading mayhem down.

Green justice being bullied
Green innocence being suffocated
Raw snake of raw power
Crawling into nooks and crannies.

Ngozi Olivia Osuoha

CONTRACTS

They give out contracts
And take their cuts
They use representatives
But they are actually the contractors.

They build inferior roads
Substandard bridges and houses
Empty estates and poor housing facilities
Cornering large monies,
The more you look
The less you see,
Green snake, dangerous creatures.

They fight for contracts
Deceiving people to believe them
But they actually fight for themselves
Milking the land very dry.

Green cobras, deadly vipers
Insane pythons, cancerous anacondas
Fear them, nothing but venomous.

CONNECTION

They connect themselves
In tables and cocktails
In parties and clubs
They ring their alarm.

In marriages, in jobs
In transfers, in postings
In promotions, in businesses
In transactions, in referrals
In all things, they connect
Just a cycle, in circle
The ring and flexibility of a snake
A green snake at that.

They hand over to their friends
Their families are their board of directors
They pledge allegiance and oath
Oath of secrecy,
They contract, covenant and bond together forever
They vow to remain in that connection.

Nothing quashes them
They build paradise for their unborn
They destroy the earth for their joy
And demolish the world for their peace,
Nothing exists except them.

Greenness of an oath
A green covenant to retain evil
Evil, typical of ungodliness
Green snake, green grass, greenly dead.

Ngozi Olivia Osuoha

ALLOCATION

They allocate wells to themselves
They allocate companies and contracts
They move monies in hard currencies
Currencies, alien to theirs.

Allocations for the masses
Allocations for the poor
To better the society
Yet they vow to make it harder.

Barrels, wells, ores, cotton, farm produce
Uncountable quotas for the people
These men evacuate them all
They invade treasuries
They loot beyond properties.

Green snake on a green grass
Drying the land
Calling forth evil upon the people
Burning hope and aspirations,
Green snakes setting green lives ablaze.

GREEN SNAKE

They are green snakes
Hiding on green grasses
Poisonous and dangerous
Callous, cancerous, corrosive.

Green, as green as grass
Deceitful, hiding their venom
Ready to attack
And attacking consciously
Killing the Innocent
Biting the ignorant
Raping the godly
Hijacking the poor.

Green snake, green grass
Pure green, lively and smart
Clever, eager, enthusiast, enthusiastic
Passionate to do evil
Parading and charading in faith
Trapping the unsuspecting folks.

Ngozi Olivia Osuoha

MANIFESTO

They talk like angels
Promising all and swearing to do all
Their manifestoes are divine
Doctored by the gods.

Their manifestoes ring bells
Sweet, like Christmas jingles
Melodies of melodious octaves
Hopeful and lively
Full of energy and strength
Strong enough to pull down mountains
But a trap, a deceitful and pretentious lie.

Manifestoes that depict evil in actual sense
Shiny demons in white robes
Dancing to hymns
Praying litanies and chanting psalms
Pretending to be Messiahs
But Judas Iscariot is a saint.

Green manifestoes cooking like potatoes
Yet red tomatoes endangering the toes
Green deceivers in bruising accolades
Monumental harlots
Monetary gains advancing
Preaching to the gullible
Manoeuvring their ways to the top
Pushing down whoever, whatever, whenever, however.

THUGS

Thugs work for them
Even when there are none
They recruit, they gather
And empower them for battle.

Thugs born of women
Talented and healthy men
Dreams and dreamers
Able-bodied young men
The ones that need push, just a little push
Youths that should be helped,
They energize them wrongly to die wrongly
And scatter their future.

Telling them lies, sweet lies
Giving them false vibes and false hopes
Promising them lie-ful truths
And truthful lies,
Charming and enchanting them
Devising dubious ways for their own ambitions
Proffering ambiguous solutions
Suggesting and instituting wasteful ways,
Ways that are outrageously impossible.

Green snakes in green clouds
Noisy, lazy, crazy, barbaric and audacious,
Audacious like their venom
Venom of woeful men.

Ngozi Olivia Osuoha

FAMILY ON CRUISE CONTROL

Their families are abroad
Abroad, cruising, enjoying
They study and school abroad
They holiday abroad
Their medicals are abroad
They vacation abroad, in fact in heaven
They do all things overseas.

But here, they strangle others
They keep others stranded
They play with destinies
And take care of their own families.

Green snakes, they poison families
They bite futures, they burn homes
They crush toes, toes of innocent wombs.

Whatever it takes for them to prosper
Wherever they may go to survive,
Anything it will cost for them to survive
Anywhere they will be safe,
No matter whose ox is gored
They do it, obtain it, go there, live it.

But the masses are here, dying
Diseases, hunger, starvation, unemployment
Lack, want and need
They live on the people.

Green Snake on a Green Grass

Their families are not thugs
They are not their security agents and bodyguards
They are not their informants and touts
Their families live in a world so close to paradise
They are waiting for time,
Time to continue from where they stopped.

Green blood of green snakes
Hidden in grasses home and abroad
Manipulating, manoeuvring, mesmerizing.

Ngozi Olivia Osuoha

TROUBLE

They cause trouble everywhere
Even at the peak of peace,
They cook lies and rumours
Especially when something does not favour them.

They gain from trouble
They cause commotion and confusion
They derive joy from unleashing terror.

Troublemakers, instigating war
Depriving people of peace
Causing deaths and harm,
Losses and losses
Challenges and grievances
Grief, pain and imbalances.

Trouble gives them honour
Honouring them is trouble,
They appear holy and saintly
They stir calm waters
And pierce restful breasts,
Nothing works with them
Except they trouble the land.

Green snakes, greenish, greening the grass
Green grass, grazing the green snake
Green snake razzling the grassroots.

GREEN GRASS

They bear snakes
Hiding terrible heads
Closing eyes that bite
Covering mouths that spit
And cutting wires that tie.

Green grass, breezy and cool
Vegetative, appearing godly and fertile
Beautiful and wonderful
Mesmerizing beauty and wonder
But underneath hides deaths and graves.

Green snake on a green grass
Green, pure green, green like pasture
Pasture for the flock
A relief to the Shepherd
But death, death, surrounding death,
Fear them, green snakes on green grasses.

Ngozi Olivia Osuoha

NATIONAL CAKE

They call it national cake
So they scramble over it
They struggle on it
So they dabble
They wobble, dribble, cuddle
The national cake, it is
Green cake of numerous futures
They eat and share,
They smuggle, explore, exploit, discover and hide.

Money, treasure, properties
Oil, whatever be it
They share among themselves
Green snakes polluting the grass,
Quaking the land.

Nobody exists except them
Whatever good, they share
Whatever golden, they squander
They rush, steal, share, loot
They divide the greenness of the land.

National cake, it is
Sweet, sweeter, sweetest
Sweeter than honey
The bees fight tooth and nail
Struggling to produce honey
They abuse, use, misuse

They transfer and alienate to their lineages
No one else matters.

Green bunch of poisoned adventurers
Voyage of discovery navigating negatively
Sailing away wonders untold.

Ngozi Olivia Osuoha

PRETENDERS

Bunch of pretenders
Smiling faces that hurt
Warm hands that kill
Speedy legs that butcher
Sour lips that condemn.

Pretenders, they are rulers and leaders
They preach, pray and bless
They suggest, commend and recommend
They command, but a band that reprimands.

Pretenders that support you facially
And kill you otherwise,
Pretenders that send you on mission
And call enemies to attack you
Pretenders, that pray for you
But actually curse you
They promise to build you up
Yet they really destroy you,
They pretend to be lovers
But they are pure haters
They dig graves, mass graves
They bury futures of nations, national futures,
Green snake on a green grass
Green snake of a green grass
Green snake from a green grass
Green snake for a green grass,
Green, greener, greenest
They take lives, lives at their bloom.

OIL

Blessed oil, pure like gold
Godly, raw and crude
Natural, beautiful and wonderful
But here it is a problem.

Oil, divine and celestial
A gift from mother nature
Resources beyond human comprehension
But it is a war here.

Strangers drink it
Foreigners harbour it
Visitors sell it
Indigenes suffer it.

Gas flaring, soot and atmospheric disaster
Many hazards and dangers
Arising from oil, this great gift
Yet they care not.

They take the proceeds and profits
They harvest the gain
The indigenes die of the diseases.

Toxic wastes from far and near
Dumped, dumping ground
Grounds for green snakes
Deals for green mambas.

Ngozi Olivia Osuoha

BLIND

They travel abroad steady
They meet great people
They see skyscrapers and towers
They see serenity and advancement
They behave well, overseas
But they trouble us home.

They go blind to infrastructures
They deny development
They breach growths
They stop progress
Yet they fly to heaven.

Blindness and deafness
Meanness and wickedness
Hate and bigotry
Vindictive, vengefulness, antagonism
Surrounding the table of leadership.

Green snake appearing same with green grass
Green grass showcasing talents on accomplices.

AGRICULTURE

When agriculture was fruitful
They enjoyed it
Now, they have sent it to the grave
Killing food production.

Palm oil was green
Now it is dead and gone
Gold, iron, tin, cocoa and cotton
Things were abundant and real
But now, they are dead.

Careless, relaxed, comfortable, unconcerned
Nonchalant, reluctant, bossy
Busy, doing nothing
Flying up and down
Cruising, enjoying life
Never seeing death
They share slaves and servants.

They killed agriculture
They killed farmers
They made away with lands
And no one questions them.

Green snakes amidst humans
Education is forgotten
Schools are dilapidated
Academics is burning down.

Ngozi Olivia Osuoha

INDUSTRIES

The colonialists tried even
They built roads and airports
Schools, industries, hospitals, telecommunications
They fought for calm
Cleanliness was seen
Sanity was there
Justice was felt
But now, all to square one.

They killed the surviving industries
They frustrated investors
The green snakes poisoned the grasses
Yet, they bite anyone around.

Industries packed up
They all died in a twinkle
Their gradual trap worked magic.

It seemed and still seems only a people involved
From the beginning, a people were victors
A certain people too were victims,
A tribe conspicuously marginalised
Intentionally frustrated and killed,
A bold frustration and killing
A black on white garment,
Snakes, snakes, snakes
They know themselves
They hide it not.

UNEMPLOYMENT

Youths are jobless
Graduates are multiplying
No work, no incentive
No supply, no demand
No support, no pat on the back
Unemployment, tracking down youths.

In their thousands, they suffer
Some get entangled with drugs
Some in alcohol, some in kidnapping
Some in robbery, some in other crimes,
Yet they are guilty even before charged.

Unemployment, a chain of evil
Connecting young and old
Linking blue blood and green eyes
Choking voices and hopes
Smashing heads and souls
Crushing dreams and futures,
Futures we pray for
A trouble that finds one and many, out.

No one to raise a finger
No hand to clap for success
No man to bear the mantle
No tribe to carry the ark of covenant,
As green snakes poison nooks and crannies.

Ngozi Olivia Osuoha

CARTEL

They run cartels and brothels
And engage the youths
Youthful lust and exuberance
Green energy being harnessed devilishly.

Cartels of uncountable deeds
Unthinkable sights and stories
Unimaginable gains and greed
Unremorseful use and abuse
Dead conscience and decayed manners
That is why and where they need youths.

Brothels, cartels, groups and classes
Boys and girls, men and women
Illicit businesses and illegal ventures
Cursed adventures and ungodly enterprises
A hole in the whole of the land.

Green skin, skin of green motives
Puncturing and perforating
Incarnating and inventing woes,
Woes upon the earth.

SCHOLARSHIP

They falsely raise scholarship
Pretending to have foundations
Non governmental organizations,
All these are more avenues
Avenues to milk the land drier.

Their scholarship is unreal
Hardly real without a selfish gain
Their foundation is untrue
Hardly true without greedy intention
They set up diverse things
Secretly and openly
They use other names
They forge and falsify
They legalize and commonize evil.

Scholarships that should help the poor
Organizations that should support the needy
They ruin the poor totally
And destroy the needy outrightly,
Satisfying their unsearchable and insatiable urge
Using the poor and needy as camouflage.

Green snakes that bite new born
Green snakes that kill green bones
Green grasses that bury green features and fractures.

Ngozi Olivia Osuoha

FALSE CONTRACTS

They award false contracts
Ingenuine contracts on paper
They spread the news all over
And share the money among themselves.

They pump money in millions
They run up and down in Syrens
Tinted cars and convoys
Entourages and securities
They intimidate all corners.

Laws are there, at their mercy
Rules belong to them, they dictate
Regulations they make, not binding on them
Above the laws, beyond reach
Butterflies and birds, colourful wings
Flying as far and wide as possible.

Serpentine grasses, abode of disguise
Grasses of mournful land
Witches and wizards;
Practising witchcraft and wizardry.

TITLES

When they become this influential
They control the lands
They dish out laws and orders
They direct traditions
They influence cultures
And they fluctuate religion.

Traditional people give them titles
Political people give them appointments
Religious people give them ordinations
Educational people give them posts,
Positions and titles chase them around
They become lords and Irokos
Nothing humbles them anymore.

All their deeds go unchecked
All their talks go unchallenged
All their behaviours become right
They force nails and weapons down throats.

Titles fly on them
They may even reject some
Titles upon titles,
Their families turn royalties
While others languish and rot,
The upright ones, at that.

Green snakes posing nude
Seducing the world
Raping souls and spirits
Offending God and mankind.

Ngozi Olivia Osuoha

COMMISSIONING FAKE PROJECTS

They commission fake projects
Childish and selfish,
Projects that are shameful
Poor and substandard
Needless and useless
They boldly commission them.

They travel in noisy Syrens
After wasting the whole day waiting
They arrive like suspects
Always in a hurry
In loud and mighty entourages
Only to commission a waste.

Monies mapped out
Yet unseen, unknown, unheard
Fake and inferior projects
Projects that spoil before and after commissioning.

RENTED CROWDS

They rent crowds
Crowds to cheer them up
They pay them peanuts
Some sustain injuries along the line
Some never receive anything,
Sometimes, heads swallow such pays.

Rented crowds, crowds so ignorant
Sometimes, they lure them to the venues with lies
You are coming for empowerment
The saviour is coming
Come and meet the Messiah and be healed
But when they get there
Lo and behold, different ball game.

They interview some
They arrange answers
They take them unawares
Just to capture and show the world
How good their supports and works are.

Deceitful men, cunning in all ways
Green snakes, fallow lies the farm.

Ngozi Olivia Osuoha

OLD STUFFS

Sometimes they sell old stuffs
Office equipments inclusive
Some loot and share among themselves.

Sometimes, they repaint them
And present them as new ones
They commission them then,
They gift them to agencies
They appear new and real
Meanwhile they have grabbed the monies,
Allocations meant for new ones and real ones.
They bought the old ones
They took the spoil
They bought the new-old ones
They fabricate whatever, anyhow
Their pocket is all that matters.

They gain from everything
They dupe, manipulate, manoeuvre
Their intent is always greed.

Green greedy lots
Determined and focused
Bent on squandering
Squandering the economy.

HIRING

When they must present something
Especially when guests are coming
Things that are necessary, necessities
They hire, they shamelessly hire;
Things that have been severally provided for.

Also, they bill for hiring, in anyway suitable
It is a money making machine,
Except death, almost nothing changes them
Perpetual workers, renewing their age.

Green snake on green grass
Corrupting the land for cultivation
Infiltratig harvest.

When someone wants it done well
They shortchange him
He pays with his life,
If he is lucky, he gets transferred.

Ngozi Olivia Osuoha

IMMUNIZATION

Many a time, millions are spent
Millions on immunization
Billed on Mother and child mortality
Yet, lives are being lost.

Simple necessary things
They play politics
They play religion
They play culture
They play tradition
They play tribe
They play connection
And the land gets bloodier.

Monies flying, wrongly channelled
Wrong hands magneting them
Greedy bellies stomaching them
Lives, sweeping away.

Green snakes on green grasses
Biting and spiting
Biting lives, spiting futures.

NEGLIGENCE

Negligence is the order
Few available facilities decaying
Properties of countless millions dilapidating
Going obsolete, into oblivion
No maintenance culture
Weeds, taking over
Schools, stadia, hospitals becoming forests,
The most they can do is to move them.

Politically, they tussle
They fight to move the few ones
They come up with cock and bull stories
Fooling themselves,
Silly and disconnected reasons
Uncoordinated and unimportant excuses,
Green masters of green anacondas.

Ngozi Olivia Osuoha

INCOMPETENCE

Nothing is by merit
Incompetent and half baked
Quarks and quarks,
Illiterates and ignorant fellows
Heading, commanding, fielding.

Influence on everything
Connection everywhere
Wrong people in wrong areas
Causing havoc and commotion
Ruining hopes
Everything upside down.

Talents wasting, gifts dying
Incompetent caretakers
Inefficient supervisors
Green, turning black.

Malpractice, misconduct
Mistreatment, mismanagement
Incompetent leaders and drivers
Leading and driving, driving and leading
Crashing those onboard.

ARRAIGNING FAKE SUSPECTS

They arraign them on the screens
Accusing and alleging against them
Suspecting them of crimes
Many a time, they are innocent.

We will bring perpetrators to book
Bail is free
Police is your friend
The accused is innocent until proven guilty
We are on top of the situation
Investigations are ongoing
In case of emergency, call the following ..:
Grammars that amaze even the dead.

Culprits at large
Cohorts, cruising
Caucus, plotting and executing.

Poor innocent victims
Voiceless, speechless, powerless
Arraigning them to take credit
Credit of a failed society.

Ngozi Olivia Osuoha

DETENTION

Of detentions that baffle
Of stories that bewilder
Rape of detainees
Extra judicial killings
Intimidation and luring.

Detained and mesmerized
Abused and misused
Within and without
Inmates and out-mates
Detention, cell of wonders.

Green snake on green grass
Burning people in a fiery furnace,
Killing the gold in them.

CRIME IS BUSINESS

Fight justly or unjustly
Gather many followers
Arm them for killings
Call for dialogue
Ask for amnesty
You will become a king.

They beg you, pay you
They pay, beg you
You give them conditions
They give you better conditions,
Their offer is green
The option is rich
Accept for awhile.

Threaten after some time
Top up the conditions
More offers are coming
More bodies involved
Cause more troubles and problems
In the end, crime is business.

Yes, crime is business
Play your card well
Lure them to dance to your tune
Vibrate and gyrate
After the killings and murdering
Your fame spreads home and abroad,
Green business of green crime.

Ngozi Olivia Osuoha

Link up with regions and subregions
Hook with some nations
The world would honour you,
Placards bring guns
Guns bring respect.

Green snakes, green grasses
Destroying green lands,
The struggle is real
The hustle is theirs,
They are tacticians
But amazing morticians.

SYNDICATES

They are syndicates
In and out, out and in
They are in power
They are in tradition
They are in religion
In security, in academia
In the street, in the society
They are everywhere.

They always get it their way
And they always get away
Arrest them, you will be arrested
Challenge them, you will be challenged
Whatever, you will blame yourself.

Green snakes under carpets
Carpets of heads of organizations
They bite, they spit, they harm
Fear them, they are syndicates.

Their boldness frightens
Their courage tells it all
Their operation, wonders
Their arm says it all,
Poor society, who bewitched thee?

Ngozi Olivia Osuoha

RITUALS

Their rituals are there
Physical, mental, spiritual, social
Religious, all round,
Unseen, but seen
Unknown, but known
Unheard, but heard
Unfelt, but felt
Secret, but open,
Green snakes crawling at midnight.

Human, animal, monetary rituals
Open secret, secret open
See them in the movies.

Humans dying mysteriously
Babies missing amazingly
Miserable lives up and down
Watch movies.

They eat human flesh
They sleep with animals
They drink blood,
Movies say it all.

BRIBERY AND CORRUPTION

Bags of hard currencies
Papers of juicy contracts
They bribe, they corrupt
Yet, they set you up.

Sometimes, they bribe, no set up
Sometimes they corrupt and contaminate
They influence everything
Even talent hunts and featuring
They make calls only, they give orders
And there ends it, it is done
They are just gods, and God
Green pepper, peppering the masses.

Their influence is heavy
Hard to decipher from others
All powers and all heads
All heads and all powers
Colluding, colliding, conniving, compounding
Outrageous power to quench mankind,
Green snake eating up the green grass.

Ngozi Olivia Osuoha

PREGNANCY

Fake pregnancy and baby bump
Injections and treatments
Treatments to blow the tommy.

Baby swapping, baby selling
Illegal adoption, abduction and stealing
Professionals of ungodly acts
Pregnancies that may last over a year
As they await a magic baby,
Abnormal, barbaric, demonic, sickening.

Hidden in the womb, or waist
Then comes a ceaserian section
When you wake up they give you a baby
A miraculous baby
A wonderment, after paying millions,
Green babies, from green snakes.

Green snakes everywhere
In families, in professions
Green deals by green snakes beyond green grass,
Evil deals, dark gains.

FALSE DIAGNOSIS

They run false diagnosis
They may call it cancer
Just to make money.

They 'treat' and burn you
They administer whatever, however
They give you trauma
They invoke death before time
Green snakes, making money.

They run different outlets
Deceiving and fooling people
Making horrible monies from men
Yet, leaving a dirty footprint with them.

False diagnosis for money
Greed, selfish desires
Material wealth and quest
Ungodly and inhumane acts
Acts destroying humanity.

Deadly snakes, fear them
Cobra of incurable venom
They harm, they poison, they kill.

Ngozi Olivia Osuoha

SORTING AND SEXUAL HARASSMENT

They dress like angels
And appear like saints
But they are the ones that fail students
Brilliant students suffer in their hands,
Yes, they fail brilliant students, females especially
Because they want to sleep with them.

Some tell them to hire hotel room
Some say it is in their office
Some say, they will travel with them
They victimize female students.

Sometimes, men fall victim
Especially if they move with their favourite girl
They may not even know.

Some sort with cash
Some sort with kind
Some are ready, some not
Some delay students for years.

Holy ones say no
Righteous ones say never
Principled and disciplined ones contemplate
These ones wonder, they pray and pray
They call on God, as some mock them,
Whatever happens, their fate hangs there.

Green snakes vomiting green venom
Bastardizing education, mesmerizing futures
Futures of bright students,
As dullards relax, waiting for sorting time
And brilliant ones go down.

DISEASES

They invent diseases
They manufacture sickness
They do laboratory findings
They research and discover
Then, they inject in mammals.

Then, they produce cures
Selling and making millions
Becoming popular, famous and influential
They rule classes and stages
They turn lords and gods
Green snakes, poisoning lives.

Look them, innocent faces
Demons at night
Spirits of death, calling upon death.

Discover the cure and die
Produce the vaccine and vanish
They trace and track you,
Green snakes crawling into you by night.

They destroy futures
They disband battalions
Green mambas flying around.

Serpents of wingless flights
Yet, flying round the world
Eating up destinies
And tormenting God.

Ngozi Olivia Osuoha

DRIVERS AND GUARDS

These ones see it all
They see, hear and go places
Phone discussions, visitors, friends, colleagues
Associates, accomplices, companions
They read bosses like paper
They know them well,
But they pretend, they keep calm
Especially those under oath.

Green snakes, they sure can harm
Times, tell
Places, tell
Events, tell.
Life goes on
Until time is up.

COOKS AND MAIDS

The ones who feed you
They cook and dish
They make your favourite
They control your appetite
And manipulate your stomach.

The power to kill
The power to poison
The power to keep,
These ones dance with them.

Green snakes with long tails
Under the roof, under the bed
Many a time, they cross boundaries.

Watch them, take heed
They have powers to undo
Except God be with you.
Innocent, poor, loyal, humble, respectful
Yes, they can be too.

Ngozi Olivia Osuoha

VISAS

They lure you with sweet poison
Beautiful package well wrapped,
Promises of greener pastures
Pastures for your unborn too.

They sell green cards
They produce visas
They give jobs
They give foreign scholarships
Visas and residency,
Their package is too good.

Green snakes, they bundle you out
From frying pan to fire
Through deserts and wilderness
Through mountains and valleys
Strange and harsh treatments
With death staring greenly at you.

Thousands taken, never returned
Hundreds returned, never speak up
They die in silence.

Green snakes making money with destinies
Arranging for slave trade
Sex trade, organ trade, human trafficking
Prostitution, crude slavery, modern slavery.

Green Snake on a Green Grass

As prayers rise up home
As hopes long beyond
As wishes tarry
As bonds shake
As wanderings go on and on,
Green snakes enjoy the labour and dirty sweat of others.

about the author

Ngozi Olivia Osuoha is a Nigerian poet, writer and thinker. A graduate of Estate Management with experience in Banking and Broadcasting.

She has published twelve poetry books and co-authored one (with Kenyan literary critic Amos O. Ojwang').

She has featured in more than forty international anthologies and also has published over two hundred and fifty poems and articles in over twenty countries.

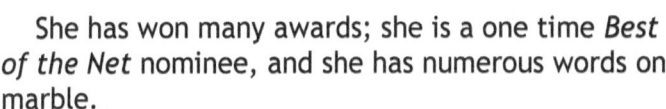

Many of her poems have been translated and published into other languages, including Spanish, Romanian, Khloe, Farsi, and Arabic, among others.

She has won many awards; she is a one time *Best of the Net* nominee, and she has numerous words on marble.

www.ingramcontent.com/pod-product-compliance
Lightning Source LLC
Chambersburg PA
CBHW030101100526
44591CB00008B/222